WHILE WE'RE HERE

Barney Norris

WHILE WE'RE HERE

OBERON BOOKS
LONDON

WWW.OBERONBOOKS.COM

First published in 2017 by Oberon Books Ltd
521 Caledonian Road, London N7 9RH
Tel: +44 (0) 20 7607 3637 / Fax: +44 (0) 20 7607 3629
e-mail: info@oberonbooks.com
www.oberonbooks.com

PB ISBN: 9781786821218
E ISBN: 9781786821225

Cover design by Studio Doug

Printed and bound by 4edge Limited, UK

For Mum and Rob.

With thanks to Emily Mclaughlin; Sarah, Gavin, Richard, Heather, Christine, house and Farnham Maltings; Vicky, Lucy, Ola, Ryan, Minna and the Royal Court; Gareth and Salisbury Playhouse; Russ and the Pound Arts Centre; Mike, Ali and the Tobacco Factory; Lucy, Sherrell, Amy and the North Wall; Sophie, Jemma, Ayad and the Spring Arts Centre; everyone we interviewed in Havant; all the actors who helped us in the workshops; Sheila, Hayden, George and Matt; Madani, Jon, Sophie, Lauren, Stewart, Lise, Rebekah, Mike and everyone at the Bush Theatre; The Corner Shop PR; George Spender and Oberon Books; Rozzy Wyatt and Judy Daish Associates; Alice, Charlie and the company.

While We're Here is supported using public funding by Arts Council England.

Project development was seeded by house, in association with the Spring Arts Centre, The North Wall, and Pound Arts.

UP IN ARMS

Artistic Directors | Alice Hamilton and Barney Norris
Resident Stage Manager | Charlie Young
Up In Arms is produced by Farnham Maltings

Honest, human, affecting, revealing: we make plays about people and the places they're from.

Up In Arms makes theatre to reveal what is extraordinary about people's ordinary lives. The company's work has featured in theatre of the year lists from *The Times, The Guardian, the Evening Standard, The Arts Desk* and *The Stage*, as well as winning numerous awards. Whether touring to the UK's leading theatres, its areas of lowest cultural engagement or communities particularly affected by issues in their work, the company's project is always the same: to engage people emotionally with the conditions of their lives and the lives being lived around them.

Our audiences make us who we are.

We'd particularly like to acknowledge the contribution of our Supporters:

Very Special Thanks to Frank and Elizabeth Brenan, Alison Lowdon, Derek Relph, Sarah, Pete and Ruth Shepherd, Peter and Jane Hamilton.

Special Thanks to Offline Magazine, Rachel Bebb, Susanna Bishop, Farhana Bhula, Shabana Bhula, Richard Broyd, John Cox, Veronica Dewan, Bekah Diamond, Hasan Dixon, Esther Ruth Elliott, John Foster, Victoria Gee, Hannah Groombridge, Anna Hamilton and Angus Meryon, Juliette Kelly-Fleming, Suzy McClintock, Alice Malin, Linda Morse, Frank Newhofer, Janet Rieder, Stephanie Ressort, Sue Snell, Celia Swan.

Thanks to the Workers Educational Association, Lindsay Balkwell and Ivan Richardson, Sarah Blake, Cassie Bradley, Sophia Chetin-Leuner, Natalie Denton, Milly Ellis, Laura Elmes, Aidan Grounds, Barbara Houseman, Luke Holbrook, Louisa Hollway, Katharine Ingle, Max Lindsay, Alex Orchard-Lisle, George Nichols, Joz Norris, Naomi Petersen, Kandy Rohmann, Carly Thoms, Josie Underwood, George Warren.

You can find out more about becoming a Supporter at **upinarms.org.uk.**

KEEP IN TOUCH – JOIN OUR MAILING LIST
Online upinarms.org.uk
Twitter @upinarmstheatre
Facebook Up In Arms
Instagram upinarmstheatre

Supported using public funding by
ARTS COUNCIL ENGLAND
LOTTERY FUNDED

Bush Theatre

We make theatre for London. Now.

The Bush is a world-famous home for new plays and an internationally renowned champion of playwrights. We discover, nurture and produce the best new writers from the widest range of backgrounds from our home in a distinctive corner of west London.

The Bush has won over 100 awards and developed an enviable reputation for touring its acclaimed productions nationally and internationally.

We are excited by exceptional new voices, stories and perspectives – particularly those with contemporary bite which reflect the vibrancy of British culture now.

Located in the newly renovated old library on Uxbridge Road in the heart of Shepherd's Bush, the theatre houses two performance spaces, a rehearsal room and the lively Library Bar.

bushtheatre.co.uk

THANK YOU
TO OUR SUPPORTERS

The Bush Theatre would like to thank all its supporters whose valuable contributions have helped us to create a platform for our future and to promote the highest quality new writing, develop the next generation of creative talent and lead innovative community engagement work.

LONE STAR

Eric Abraham
Gianni Alen-Buckley
Michael Alen-Buckley
Rafael & Anne-Helene Biosse Duplan
Garvin & Steffanie Brown
Rob & Siri Cope
Miles Morland

HANDFUL OF STARS

Dawn & Gary Baker
Sofia Barattieri
Martin Bartle
Richard & Lucille Briance
Charlie Bigham
Clive & Helena Butler
Clare & Chris Clark
Clyde Cooper
Alice Findlay
Zarina Funk
Richard & Jane Gordon
Vera Monotti Graziadei
Madeleine Hodgkin
Priscilla John
Simon & Katherine Johnson
Philippa Seal & Philip Jones QC
V&F Lukey
Georgia Oetker
Philip & Biddy Percival
Robert Rooney
Joana & Henrik Schliemann
Lesley Hill & Russ Shaw
Team Nelson
and one anonymous donor.

RISING STARS

ACT IV
Nicholas Alt
Mark Bentley
David Brooks
Simon Burstein
Matthew Byam Shaw
Jennifer Caruso Viall
Tim & Andrea Clark
Sarah Clarke
Claude & Susie Cochin de Billy
Lois Cox
Matthew Cushen
Andrew & Amanda Duncan
Natalie Fellowes & Simon Gresham Jones
Lady Antonia Fraser
Jack Gordon & Kate Lacy
Hugh & Sarah Grootenhuis

RISING STARS CONTINUED

Thea Guest
Mary Harvey
Ann & Ravi Joseph
Davina & Malcolm Judelson
Cathy & Paul Kafka
Miggy Littlejohns
Isabella Macpherson
Liz & Luke Mayhew
Michael McCoy
Judith Mellor
Caro Millington
Mark & Anne Paterson
Barbara Prideaux
Emily Reeve
Renske & Marion
Sarah Richards
Sophie Silocchi
Susie Saville Sneath
Saleem & Alexandra Siddiqi
Brian Smith
Nick Starr
Peter Tausig
Lady Marina Vaizey
Guy Vincent & Sarah Mitchell
Amanda Waggott
Sir Robert & Lady Wilson
Peter Wilson-Smith & Kat Callo
Alison Winter
and three anonymous donors.

SPONSORS & SUPPORTERS

AKA
Alen-Buckley LLP
Gianni & Michael Alen-Buckley
Jeremy Attard Manche
Bill & Judy Bollinger
Edward Bonham Carter
Martin Bowley
Duke & Duchess of Buccleuch
The Hon Mrs Louise Burness
Sir Charles & Lady Isabella Burrell
Philip & Tita Byrne
CHK Charities Limited
Peppe & Quentin Ciardi
Joanna & Hadyn Cunningham
Leo & Grega Daly
Patrick & Mairead Flaherty
Sue Fletcher
The Hon Sir Rocco Forte
The Hon Portia Forte
Mark Franklin
The Right Hon Piers Gibson
Farid & Emilie Gragour
Victoria Gray
John Gordon

SPONSORS & SUPPORTERS CONTINUED

Vivienne Guinness
Melanie Hall
Lesley Hill & Russ Shaw
Madeleine Hodgkin
Michael Holland & Denise O'Donoghue
Graham & Amanda Hutton
James Gorst Architects Ltd.
Simon & Katherine Johnson
Bernard Lambilliotte
The Lord Forte Foundation
Peter & Bettina Mallinson
Mahoro Charitable Trust
Mitsui Fodosan (U.K.) Ltd
Alfred Munkenbeck III
Nick Hern Books
RAB Capital
Josie Rourke
Kevin Pakenham
Tim & Catherine Score
Search Foundation
Richard Sharp
Susie Simkins
Edward Snape & Marilyn Eardley
Michael & Sarah Spencer
Stanhope PLC
Ross Turner
The Syder Foundation
van Tulleken Family
Johnny & Dione Verulam
Robert & Felicity Waley-Cohen
Westfield London
Phillip Wooller
Danny Wyler
and three anonymous donors.

TRUSTS AND FOUNDATIONS

The Andrew Lloyd Webber Foundation
The Bruce Wake Charitable Trust
The City Bridge Trust
Cockayne—Grants for the Arts
The John S Cohen Foundation
The Daisy Trust
The Equity Charitable Trust
Eranda Rothschild Foundation
Esmée Fairbairn Foundation
Fidelio Charitable Trust
Foyle Foundation
Garfield Weston Foundation
Garrick Charitable Trust

TRUSTS AND FOUNDATIONS CONTINUED

The Gatsby Charitable Foundation
The Harold Hyam Wingate Foundation
Hammersmith United Charities
Heritage of London Trust
The Idlewild Trust
John Lyon's Charity
The J Paul Getty Jnr Charitable Trust
The John Thaw Foundation
The Leche Trust
The Leverhulme Trust
The London Community Foundation
Margaret Guido's Charitable Trust
The Martin Bowley Charitable Trust
The Monument Trust
Paul Hamlyn Foundation
Pilgrim Trust
The Theatres Trust
Viridor Credits
The Williams Charitable Trust
Western Riverside Environmental Fund
The Wolfson Foundation
and one anonymous donor.

CORPORATE SPONSORS & MEMBERS

The Agency (London) Ltd
Dorsett Shepherds Bush
Drama Centre London
The Groucho Club
THE HOXTON

PUBLIC FUNDING

If you are interested in finding out how to be involved, please visit the 'Support Us' section of bushtheatre.co.uk or email **development@bushtheatre.co.uk** or call **020 8743 3584**

farnham **maltings**

Farnham Maltings is a cultural organisation that works with artists and communities of South East England to encourage the most people to make the best art they can. We believe that the arts help us to make sense of the world, bring people together and articulate new ideas. By encouraging people to participate in the arts, as audiences and makers, we will foster a healthier, happier and safer contemporary Britain.

We are curious about how we make and build an audience for contemporary theatre. We support a network of 180 venues across the region, organise a bi-annual showcase of new English performance for an international audience, produce a stable of independent theatre companies and are working to diversify the makers and audience for the arts.

  farnhammaltings.com

Farnham Maltings is a registered charity (no 305034) supported by Arts Council England and Waverly Borough Council.

While We're Here 2017 Tour Dates

April 26th – May 27th
BUSH THEATRE, LONDON
bushtheatre.co.uk | 020 8743 5050

June 5th – 8th
THE NORTH WALL ARTS CENTRE, OXFORD
thenorthwall.com | 01865 319450

June 9th – 10th
TOBACCO FACTORY THEATRES, BRISTOL
tobaccofactorytheatres.com | 0117 902 0344

June 13th – 14th
THE SPRING ARTS CENTRE, HAVANT
thespring.co.uk | 023 9247 2700

June 15th – 17th
SALISBURY PLAYHOUSE
salisburyplayhouse.com | 01722 320 333

Company Biographies

Beth Absalom | Assistant Stage Manager
Theatre includes: *Wonderland* (UK Tour), *Saving Jason* (Park Theatre), *Affection* (Outbox Theatre), *Robinson Crusoe* (Musical Theatre Academy).
Beth has recently graduated from the Royal Central School of Speech and Drama.

Dom Coyote | Composer and Sound Designer
Theatre as composer includes: *As The Crow Flies* (Pentabus), *The Borrowers* (Sherman Cymru), *Watership Down* (Watermill Theatre), *Minotaur, The Caucasian Chalk Circle* (Unicorn Theatre), *The Night Before Christmas* (West Yorkshire Playhouse), *Clause 39* (Salisbury Cathedral), *Extraordinary Bodies* (Cirque Bijou/Diverse City), *Kes* (CAST), *Bridging The Gap* (Bristol Green Capital).
Theatre as Lead Artist includes: *Songs for the End of the World* (Battersea Arts Centre/West Yorkshire Playhouse/UK tour), *The Story Fishers* (National Theatre), *Cape Sound Stories* (Haus der Kulturen, Berlin), *Folk In A Box* (Sydney Festival/Venice Biennale).
Dom is an associate artist of Kneehigh Theatre.

Sally Ferguson | Lighting Designer
For Farnham Maltings: *Jess And Joe Forever* (Orange Tree).
Other theatre includes: *The Two Boroughs Project* (Young Vic), *Sweet Charity* (Manchester Royal Exchange), *We Wait In Joyful Hope, And Then Come The Nightjars, Many Moons* (Theatre 503), *Shiver, Lost In Yonkers* (Watford Palace Theatre), *The Sleeping Beauties* (Sherman Cymru), *As You Like It, Floyd Collins* (Southwark Playhouse), *Hag, The Girl With The Iron Claws* (Wrong Crowd/Soho Theatre), *Microcosm* (Soho Theatre), *The Imagination Museum* (UK tour), *Slowly* (Riverside Studios), *Cosi fan Tutte* (Village Underground), *The Devils Festival* (The Print Room), *The Marriage Of Figaro* (Wilton's Music Hall), *The Wonder! A Woman Keeps A Secret* (BAC).

Andrew French | Eddie
For the Bush: *I Like Mine With A Kiss.*
Theatre includes: *This Flesh Is Mine, When Nobody Returns* (Border Crossings), *The Iphigenia Quartet* (Gate Theatre), *The Merchant Of Venice* (Almeida), *Boi Boi Is Dead, Refugee Boy* (West Yorkshire Playhouse),

The Roundabout Season (Paines Plough), *Julius Caesar* (RSC), *Monster* (Manchester Royal Exchange), *As You Like It* (Wyndham's), *Reference to Salvador Dali* (Arcola/ Young Vic), *The Taming Of The Shrew, The Tempest* (Nottingham Playhouse), *The Merchant of Venice, Troilus and Cressida* (National Theatre), *The Merchant of Venice* (Shakespeare's Globe), *Things Fall Apart* (West Yorkshire Playhouse/Royal Court), *The Tempest* (Shared Experience).

Film includes: *Artificial Horizon, Breaking the Bank, Song for Marion, Exorcist: The Beginning, Exorcist: Dominion, The Merchant of Venice, Doctor Sleep, The Tailor of Panama.*

Television includes: *Capital, Eastenders, Holby City, Doctors, Perfect Parents, Primeval, Soundproof, Blast!, The Bill, Trust, In Deep, A Touch of Frost, Casualty, Family Affairs, Burnside, Tough Love.*

Radio includes: *The Mother Of..., The Last Supper.*

Alice Hamilton | Director
Direction at the Bush: *Visitors* (Up In Arms, also Arcola and tour).
Other direction for Up In Arms: *German Skerries* (Orange Tree and tour), *Eventide* (Arcola and tour), *Fear Of Music* (tour with Out of Joint), *At First Sight* (tour and Latitude Festival).
Other theatre includes: *Echo's End* (Salisbury Playhouse), *Orca* (Papatango), *Thirty Christmases* (Supporting Wall), *Orson's Shadow* (Southwark Playhouse) and Staff Director on *Man And Superman* (National Theatre).

Ashley Illman | Deputy Stage Manager
Theatre includes: *Room on the Broom, The Gruffalo's Child, Alfie White: Space Explorer, Emily Brown and the Thing* (Tall Stories), *#ChipShoptheMusical* (Emma Hill Writes, Freedom Studios, Bolton Octagon), *Kingmaker* (St James Theatre), *Showstopper!* (UK tour), *I Can Cook Live* (Endemol), *Care Of Henry, Robin's Winter Adventure* (Pied Piper Theatre), *The Big Catwalk, Wild About Phones* (Watford Palace Theatre), *Done To Death* (Soho Theatre), *Bassett* (Belgrade Theatre), *Oliver Reed: Wild Thing, Hardeep Singh Kohli's Indian Takeaway* (Seabright Productions), *Blue Surge* (Finborough), *The Coronation of Poppea* (OperaUpClose), *Bent, New Boy, The Lonesome West* (Tabard Theatre), *Dr Korczak's Example* (Arcola).

Barney Norris | Writer

Plays at the Bush: *Visitors* (Up In Arms, also Arcola and tour).

Other plays for Up In Arms: *Eventide* (Arcola and tour), *Fear Of Music* (tour with Out of Joint), *At First Sight* (tour and Latitude Festival).

Other plays: *Echo's End, Every You Every Me* (Salisbury Playhouse).

Barney is the author of a novel, *Five Rivers Met On A Wooded Plain*, and a book on theatre, *To Bodies Gone: The Theatre of Peter Gill*.

Tessa Peake-Jones | Carol

For the Bush: *Crossing The Equator*.

Theatre includes: *Beacons* (Park Theatre), *Home, Brimstone and Treacle* (Arcola Theatre), *Park Avenue Cat* (Arts Theatre London), *The Five Wives of Maurice Pinder* (National Theatre), *Shirley Valentine* (Haymarket Theatre Basingstoke), *The Park, Hamlet, A Comedy Of Errors* (RSC), *Pride and Prejudice* (Leicester Haymarket/Old Vic), *The Misanthrope, The Vortex, The Beaux' Stratagem* (Cambridge Theatre Company), *Romeo and Juliet* (Birmingham Rep), *Quartermaine's Terms, Ring Round The Moon* (Bristol Old Vic), *The Winter's Tale* (Thorndike Theatre).

Film includes: *Bonobo, The Devil Went To Islington, First Night*.

Television includes: *Grantchester, Unforgotten, Midsomer Murders, Marchlands, Doctor Who, Legacy, Poirot, Doctors, Heartbeat, Poppy Shakespeare, Dalziel and Pascoe, Lost World, Waking The Dead, Holby City, Fish, A Summer In The Suburbs, Births, Marriages and Deaths, Tom Jones, Only Fools And Horses, The Demon Headmaster, So Haunt Me, Up The Garden Path, The Bell, Anything More Would Be Greedy, Two Gentlemen of Verona, Stick With Me Kid, Iphigenia At Aulis, Quartermaine's Terms, What The Butler Saw, The Soldier, When We Are Married, Strangers And Brothers, Keeping Score, Charters And Caldicott, Pride And Prejudice, Danedyke Mystery, Telford's Change, Casualty, The Bill, Hard Cases*.

Tessa loves making radio plays and formed a company called Tight Assets Theatre with Gillian Bevan and Helen Kluger.

James Perkins | Designer

With Up In Arms: *German Skerries* (Orange Tree and tour), *Eventide* (Arcola and tour).

For the Bush: *Ciphers* (Out of Joint).

For Farnham Maltings: *Jess and Joe Forever* (Orange Tree).

Other theatre credits include: *Skylight* (Theatr Clwyd), *Sweet Charity, Little Shop Of Horrors* (Royal Exchange, Manchester), *Pilgrims* (Hightide, Theatr Clwyd, Yard Theatre), *The Last Five Years* (New Wolsey Theatre), *The Gathered Leaves* (Park Theatre), *Breeders* (St James Theatre), *Shiver, Lost In Yonkers* (Watford Palace Theatre), *1001 Nights* (Unicorn Theatre/Transport Theatre), *Liar Liar* (Unicorn Theatre), *The Girl In The Yellow Dress* (Salisbury Playhouse), *Microcosm* (Soho Theatre), *Dances Of Death* (Gate Theatre), *The Fantasist's Waltz* (York Theatre Royal), *Stockwell* (Tricycle Theatre), *Carthage, Foxfinder, Events While Guarding The Bofors Gun, Trying* (Finborough Theatre), *The Only True History Of Lizzie Finn, Floyd Collins* (Southwark Playhouse), *The Marriage Of Figaro* (Wilton's Music Hall), *Life Of Stuff, Desolate Heaven, Threads, Many Moons* (Theatre503), *The Pirates of Penzance, HMS Pinafore* (Buxton Opera House). James created *Story Whores*. He is an associate of Forward Theatre Project and one third of paper/scissors/stone.

Jasmine Sandalli | Production Manager

With Up In Arms: *Visitors* (Arcola, Bush and tour).

Theatre as Production Manager includes: *Splendour* (Donmar Warehouse), *This House*, 10 plays for *Connections 2013* (National Theatre); *Sweeney Todd, Rags, Little Women, A Man Of No Importance, A Catered Affair* and *Little Me* (Royal Academy of Music); *Cinderella* (Warwick Arts Centre); *The Hairy Ape* (Southwark Playhouse); *The Jitterbug Blitz* and *Contains Violence* (Lyric Theatre Hammersmith). Theatre as Deputy Production Manager includes: *One Man, Two Guvnors* (National Theatre; Adelphi Theatre, UK Tour); *The Kitchen, Last of the Haussmans, A Woman Killed With Kindness, Season's Greetings, Hansel and Gretel, Holy Rosenbergs* (National Theatre); *Ghost Stories, Comedians, Punk Rock, Spring Awakening* and *Metamorphosis* (Lyric Hammersmith). Jasmine is currently Production Manager for NT Live and has managed live cinema broadcasts of *Hamlet* from the Barbican, *Hangmen* and *No Man's Land* from the Wyndham's Theatre, *Amadeus* and *The Threepenny Opera* from the Olivier Theatre and *Les Liaisons Dangereuses* from the Donmar Warehouse, among others.

Victoria Smart | Costume Supervisor

Theatre with Up In Arms: *German Skerries* (Orange Tree Theatre and tour).

Theatre includes: *Carnival Journeys* (V&A/Complicite), *The Last March* (Exeter Bikeshed/Southwark Playhouse), *Maria 1968* (Edinburgh Fringe), *Enduring Song* (Southwark Playhouse), *Billy Chickens is a Psychopath Superstar* (Theatre 503 at Latitude). As associate: *Hysteria* (London Classic Theatre), *Pilgrims* (Theatr Clwyd/High Tide/Vicky Graham Productions), *Jess and Joe Forever* (Orange Tree Theatre), *P'yongyang* (Finborough Theatre), *Oliver!* (Leicester Curve), *Life Of Stuff* (Theatre 503).

Film includes: *Nether, Transition.*

Victoria is part of an artist's co-operative at Lewisham Arthouse. www.victoria-smart.tumblr.com

Charlie Young | Company Stage Manager

For the Bush: *Visitors* (Up In Arms, also Arcola and tour).

Other theatre with Up In Arms: *German Skerries* (Orange Tree and tour), *Eventide* (Arcola and tour), *Fear Of Music* (tour with Out of Joint).

For Farnham Maltings: *Miss Caledonia* (house tour).

Other theatre includes: *Room On The Broom, The Gruffalo's Child* (Kenny Wax Entertainment/Tall Stories), *The Snail and the Whale, Emily Brown and the Thing, The Snow Dragon* (Tall Stories), *The Tiger Who Came To Tea* (Nick Brooke Productions), *Barbican Box* (Barbican), *Between Us* (Arcola), *Hag, The Girl With The Iron Claws* (The Wrong Crowd), *Jesus Christ Superstar* (Bronowski Productions), *Third Floor* (Trafalgar Studios), *The Hairy Ape* (Southwark Playhouse).

While We're Here was first presented by Up In Arms, the Bush Theatre and Farnham Maltings on April 26th, 2017, with the following company:

Andrew French – EDDIE
Tessa Peake-Jones – CAROL

Director, Alice Hamilton
Designer, James Perkins
Lighting Designer, Sally Ferguson
Composer and Sound Designer, Dom Coyote
Costume Supervisor, Victoria Smart
Production Manager, Jasmine Sandalli
Company Stage Manager, Charlie Young
Deputy Stage Manager, Ashley Illman
Assistant Stage Manager, Beth Absalom
Producer, Sarah Wilson-White for Farnham Maltings

Characters

CAROL

EDDIE

The islands feel the enclasping flow,

And then their endless bounds they know.

Matthew Arnold, *To Marguerite – Continued*

The sitting room of CAROL's house. CAROL and EDDIE are making up a bed on the sofa. CAROL is sorting out a sheet. EDDIE is doing the duvet. His system, inevitably, involves getting inside the duvet cover with the duvet for a bit.

EDDIE: There was this deer, this doe, came and spied on me sometimes when I was sleeping. I'd catch her, looking at the tent when I woke up, stuck my head out. She'd look at me for a minute, then run.

CAROL: Beautiful, deer. Dapply aren't they.

EDDIE: Only at certain times of year.

CAROL: Yeah, course, when they're babies. Then they get antlers.

EDDIE: Only the males.

CAROL: Yeah, course. Like cows.

EDDIE: I use to try to work out why she looked at me. Was she afraid? Did she think I could be a source of food? Or just one animal's curiosity about another, you know?

CAROL: I don't know Eddie.

EDDIE: No. That's what's beautiful isn't it. You just look in their eyes, you know? And that's all you see.

CAROL: What on earth are you doing?

EDDIE: This is how I do it.

CAROL: I don't think it's how anyone else does it.

EDDIE: Works for me. You gotta do things how you do 'em, Carol, that's what I've found. This is a good duvet, this one.

CAROL: Leanne always used to complain the house was cold.

CAROL has finished with the sheet and moves onto the pillowcases. In a moment EDDIE will have finished with the duvet; he moves onto the pillowcases too.

CAROL: Do you have a favourite animal?

EDDIE: Guess.

CAROL: Guess your favourite animal?

EDDIE: Yeah.

CAROL: I don't know. Cows.

EDDIE: No. Whose favourite animals is cows? I like otters best. I used to say, what I really want to do, I want to make a TV show called What a Lotta Otters. Isn't that the best title you ever heard? And it would pretend to be like, a documentary, me going round the world looking at the three main different types of otters. So I'd go to Ireland and look at that kind of otter, yeah? Standard otter. And you'd see otters holding hands and swimming on their back and whatever. I'd interview a fucking otter farmer or something. And then I'd go to the Arctic. And I'd tell you, to camera, the Arctic otter has ten thousand hairs per square inch of its body. Isn't that amazing? And we'd look at them for a bit. But then, two episodes in, right, the TV show would change. Its true purpose would be revealed. I'd go to Brazil to find an Amazonian otter. You know those?

CAROL: I don't think so, no.

EDDIE: They grow up to two metres long. Bigger than us. Yeah? Amazing. Absolutely – in a fight, they will fuck up a crocodile. Yeah. Best animal. And for the final show I'd just go searching. I'd just look for one and get more and more desperate, and more and more mad. And I'd be on camera going like, whoa! Whoa! People'd be scared. And then the show would end, and I'd have told you everything you need to know about Amazonian otters. To camera. While I was mad. But we wouldn't have seen one. And people would realise, that wasn't a show about otters at all. They'd talk about it afterwards, they'd say. I know. It was a show about something else.

CAROL: What would it be about?

EDDIE: Well there you go. That's the mystery, isn't it? That's the adventure.

CAROL: I don't think people would get that.

EDDIE: No?

CAROL: There we go. That's all right isn't it.

EDDIE: It's brilliant.

CAROL: I'm sorry. I don't really go in her room that much, if I'd known she'd left it in such a state.

EDDIE: Don't be silly.

CAROL: I'll sort it all out when there's time and you can be in there, but there's no point doing it tonight if you don't mind.

EDDIE: I'm just so grateful to you Carol, you're so kind.

CAROL: It's nothing. It's a pleasure.

EDDIE: Leanne must be a proper grown up now.

CAROL: Oh, yeah.

EDDIE: Where does it go right?

CAROL: Flies by, yeah.

EDDIE: Except when you get a moment like today. Then it's like there hasn't been any time ever happened at all, or you've circled back somehow. I saw you it was like you were walking up out of the past.

CAROL: Yeah, I know. So funny. I'd only gone out for a breath of fresh.

EDDIE: Yeah.

CAROL: When Leanne still lived here I used to meet her in that park Saturdays, so we could have our lunch together, so I suppose I just wandered out thinking about Leanne.

EDDIE: Oh right?

CAROL: She worked part time in the Wilko's by there, on the tills. Half the year. The other half the year she'd move to do the camps on Hayling, that's where she's moved now, which she really loves, so.

EDDIE: That's great.

CAROL: She loves it, yeah. Really happy doing that.

EDDIE: That's really great for her.

CAROL: I met you off the bus there one time, didn't I, remember?

EDDIE: Oh my God, yeah.

CAROL: And you took me into Gregg's and bought me an apple turnover to say sorry cos you were late, and you bought a packet of custard donuts for yourself and promised you'd ration them, and I knew you wouldn't.

EDDIE: Sounds like me. So you said you were still at the council?

CAROL: I've got a job in electoral registration now, yeah.

EDDIE: No way.

CAROL: Yeah.

EDDIE: What job?

CAROL: Team leader.

EDDIE: What's that mean, that good?

CAROL: It's like manager. I'm like, head of electoral registration for Havant, actually.

EDDIE: All of Havant?

CAROL: Yeah.

EDDIE: Is that as good as it sounds?

CAROL: It is quite good, yeah.

EDDIE: I thought so, I fucking knew so! You can tell from the sound of it, I could tell that was good. Well played mate, well done.

CAROL: It's more stress than anything, really.

EDDIE: How did it happen, how come you've got such a good job? I mean, I don't mean to be rude –

CAROL: I just fell into it, to be honest. Obviously I was doing the invoicing in the depot –

EDDIE: You were good at it.

CAROL: Well.

EDDIE: Worked in the bank.

CAROL: That was my career, yeah. You remember a lot, don't you?

EDDIE: I remember everything.

CAROL: Really?

EDDIE: Total recall.

CAROL: Bloody hell.

EDDIE: Just a skill I've got.

CAROL: Well.

EDDIE: I'm distracting you. You were telling me how you got your job.

CAROL: Oh yeah. Well I just, I don't know whether you remember but when we first knew each other –

EDDIE: Your husband had left you.

CAROL: Total recall. Well I was doing whatever bit extra I could find, for money, like, and someone asked me to do some canvassing.

EDDIE: To be an MP?

CAROL: What?

EDDIE: That's when you knock on doors?

CAROL: Sometimes, but this was easier. This was just that every time you have an electoral registration signup, everyone has to get a signup form through their letterbox, see? So they can take part. And in Havant, cos it's all so close together, it's not all little villages or whatever, is it, it's cheaper to pay someone to post them by hand than send them through the post. So they hire thirty-six people to post all these forms in their evenings and weekends, that's how many people you need to do the borough. And that's the sort of canvassing I did.

EDDIE: Okay.

CAROL: They give the work to council people first off, cos it's not a proper job, it's just a few evenings, they just need it done.

EDDIE: I could do it?

CAROL: Absolutely, yeah.

EDDIE: Good to know. I'd ask you probably. If I wanted that job.

CAROL: Yeah, if we had a vacancy.

EDDIE: Good to know.

CAROL: And then I was doing that, and after a while I was asked if I wanted to join the electoral registration team. It's a team of three, a sort of part-timer at the bottom, which was me, then a deputy team leader, then a team leader. And when I joined it was Wendy was team leader and Irene was deputy and I was part-time, and then I was deputy and Irene was boss, and now it's my turn being team leader and the funny thing is that it's quite three musketeers, because Wendy's actually come back to do the part-time job now the leader's me!

EDDIE: Isn't that funny!

CAROL: Well, no, I suppose it's not really, is it, but. We meet sometimes with Irene for lunch.

EDDIE: I see the irony of it. How small the world.

CAROL: How small the world indeed.

EDDIE: You mean us?

CAROL: What?

EDDIE: Bumping into each other?

CAROL: I was just repeating you.

EDDIE: Oh. Maybe I meant us then. Must have done. Cos when you said that just then, you know. I thought of us.

CAROL: That must be it then. You said you're a recycler now, that right?

EDDIE: That's sort of it.

CAROL: Not for the council though?

EDDIE: No, don't really want a proper job right now, it'd be too – I just met this bloke in a pub did some work for a scrap yard. He gives me work cash in hand if I help out, keep me ticking over. That's why I came over this way, see.

CAROL: That sounds interesting.

EDDIE: It's all right.

CAROL: Shall we have one more drink? Seeing as we're settling you in. Celebrating your arrival.

EDDIE: Yeah, why not?

CAROL: All right.

CAROL exits to get a bottle of wine. EDDIE very quickly changes out of the clothes he's wearing, into a new t shirt he pulls out of his bag, getting it on just as CAROL re-enters.

CAROL: *(Off.)* I had a good title for a story once. Like your otter title.

EDDIE: Yeah?

CAROL: 'Everything's Battered In Bournemouth.'

EDDIE: Oh yeah?

CAROL: 'Everything's Battered In Bournemouth', yeah. It'd be a telly, about a fight that breaks out in a chip shop on a stormy night in Bournemouth, in 2008, you know, while the recession's really kicking in. And the woman behind the counter's in an abusive relationship. Every type of battered you can have, in one show, all rolled in together, and you really sort of see what's happening in the country. I think it'd star Olivia Colman.

EDDIE: Yeah.

CAROL: Or Sarah Lancashire.

EDDIE: I don't know her.

CAROL: They're both good.

EDDIE: You've thought about it quite a lot, haven't you.

CAROL enters.

CAROL: I have, actually, yeah. You've changed.

EDDIE: Well, everyone changes if you know 'em long enough.

CAROL: Your clothes.

EDDIE: I know. I was doing a funny joke.

CAROL: Very quick.

EDDIE: That's what all the nice girls tell me.

CAROL: Here you go.

EDDIE: Thanks. Why Bournemouth then?

CAROL: Alliterated. You'd be good on the telly.

EDDIE: Yeah?

CAROL: Charismatic.

EDDIE: I never really watch any TV any more.

CAROL: I suppose you can't, living as you did.

EDDIE: Exactly.

CAROL: You must miss out on so much.

EDDIE: The news.

CAROL: More important things than the news, the TV, all the TV. I don't know how you cope.

EDDIE: Sometimes I have to sit out chats at work.

CAROL: I bet you do. You can watch mine now.

EDDIE: I don't think I'd like it to be honest.

CAROL: Why not?

EDDIE: I don't know. The thought of loads of people all sitting watching the same thing at once. Like babies. I dunno. I've got enough in my head.

EDDIE sits down on the sofa.

CAROL: Is it comfy?

EDDIE: It's great. Everything's great.

CAROL: Good. I'm glad. It's gonna be nice having someone else in the house again.

EDDIE: Well hopefully I won't be under your feet for too long, you know.

CAROL: Don't think about it, it's fine. You can stay for as long as you need. Leanne probably won't come home till Christmas, she's so busy with work, so I'm on my own in the house till then.

EDDIE: Well I'll stay for as long as I can if the food's that good.

CAROL: It was good, wasn't it.

EDDIE: Yeah.

CAROL: Got it off Saturday Kitchen.

EDDIE: Oh yeah?

CAROL: Great source of inspiration, Saturday Kitchen.

EDDIE: I don't know it.

CAROL: We'll watch it together, you'll love the omelette challenge.

EDDIE: I don't think we ever had dinner together, did we. Think this was our first time.

CAROL: Wasn't really that sort of friendship, was it.

EDDIE: I'd like it if it was.

CAROL: Yes. So would I.

EDDIE: Hm.

CAROL: What?

EDDIE: Wouldn't you give anything just to go back?

CAROL: What d'you mean?

EDDIE: And have it again. To the start, even just to have the last five minutes again. Isn't it sad? And lovely, but. Wouldn't you do anything?

CAROL: You mean you and me?

EDDIE: No, I just mean being young.

CAROL: I guess so, yeah. I don't know. Where were you sleeping before, exactly?

EDDIE: Over towards Emsworth.

CAROL: Oh yeah? Nice in Emsworth.

EDDIE: Yeah.

CAROL: I used to think if I moved again I'd try to move to Emsworth, because it's not really so much of a commute when you think about it, if the trade off's being somewhere nice. But the cost. And it's not like I'd go back to renting now, and maybe I wouldn't be able to afford that either, I don't know, I haven't looked, I suppose I could look online. But wouldn't it be nice to drive to work past an oyster farm, wouldn't you feel la di da? It must have been terrible out there for you though, of course you didn't care about the oysters.

EDDIE: No, no. It's all right. Layer up if it's cold. It's not a thing. I'm just in between – defensible living arrangements, that's all, it's not a tragedy. It's only till I sort my plan.

CAROL: Your plan?

EDDIE: For my future, you know? I have actually got a bit of a plan brewing about where I'll go next, you see.

CAROL: Oh right?

EDDIE: D'you wanna hear it?

CAROL: Go on then.

EDDIE: D'you think you're ready for it?

CAROL: Sod off then.

EDDIE: No, no, sorry. I'll tell you. Rewilding.

CAROL: What?

EDDIE: That's what I'm gonna do. Rewilding.

CAROL: What's that?

EDDIE: Have you not heard of it?

CAROL: I don't know.

EDDIE: Big thing.

CAROL: Isn't it when they reintroduce wolves to Scotland?

EDDIE: That's it.

CAROL: I know about that. It's shipping beavers back to England and whatever.

EDDIE: Yeah. That's, yeah. It's about restoring historic habitats. Ecosystems, innit. The balance of things. It's rewilding the countryside, ecological – you know you press edit undo on computers? It's that, for nature.

CAROL: Why do you want to do that?

EDDIE: Why?

CAROL: Yeah.

EDDIE: Because it's amazing! You know what the same kind of work did to the red kite population in Oxfordshire?

CAROL: Something good?

EDDIE: Exactly! And that's brilliant, isn't it.

CAROL: Do we want to increase the number of wolves in Scotland?

EDDIE: The question is, do we have the right to have removed them in the first place? Maybe, right, instead of making all this fucking mess, ought we to be pressing edit undo on what we've done, you know?

CAROL: Right.

EDDIE: No?

CAROL: Well you can't press edit undo on the world, can you, that's not possible.

EDDIE: It's a manner of speaking. It's about balance, that's the thing.

CAROL: So what are you actually going to do?

EDDIE: Well, there are these charities. Really doing it, you know? Mostly up north, you know, mostly Scotland. There's more room there to get stuff done.

CAROL: Where the wild things are.

EDDIE: Yeah. And it's really busy up there, you know, it's really happening. So I'm thinking I'm gonna go up there and be part of it.

CAROL: Do they have jobs going?

EDDIE: Well a lot of it, it's more like a volunteering network at first, sort of thing. But that's how all these things start. You get your foot in the door, you work a bit for free, you meet the right people, you carve something out for yourself. That's how it happens. Bish bash bosh.

CAROL: Okay.

EDDIE: Exciting right?

CAROL: Yeah.

EDDIE: It's about putting the wonder back into things.

CAROL: Rewondering!

EDDIE: Yeah, man, yeah. You get it? You're walking along, you're in Scotland, I don't know why, but you're up a hill, you see a wolf or a boar or a bear or whatever. Imagine that!

CAROL: And you think that would make people recycle more? If there were bears?

EDDIE: It seems less exciting now I'm saying it to you.

CAROL: Is this the first time you've said all this out loud?

EDDIE: I've looked into it, it's not off the top of my head.

CAROL: No, of course. But sometimes when you say things out loud, you realise –

EDDIE: That it's a shit idea?

CAROL: No, course not. Maybe just what the challenges are.

EDDIE: Yeah, maybe.

CAROL: I don't mean to be negative.

EDDIE: Well.

CAROL: Sorry.

EDDIE: 'S all right.

CAROL: It sounds like quite an isolated sort of work.

EDDIE: I wouldn't mind that.

CAROL: No?

EDDIE: I'm usually best off keeping to myself.

CAROL: Oh yeah.

EDDIE: I don't really like people, I don't think. Best song title ever: Slipknot. People equal shit.

CAROL: Oh.

EDDIE: That's always struck a chord with me, you know. I'm like Tony Adams.

CAROL: Yeah?

EDDIE: When he was manager of Portsmouth he said if it was up to him, he'd never talk to anyone. He'd walk his dogs and have his lunch, and that'd be it.

CAROL: That'd be too lonely for me.

EDDIE: Maybe. Or maybe just peaceful.

CAROL: I don't think it's very peaceful being on your own.

EDDIE: Well. You haven't got a dog.

CAROL: No. I worry what it would be like when you had to put them down.

EDDIE: Yeah. Warm day, wasn't it. For the time of year.

CAROL: Oh, yeah, it was, yeah.

EDDIE: I like it this month. Every time it comes round. If you had to imagine what the main time for getting dark was, right, in England, the normal time, I know it changes all year but if you had to pick one, that was like, the centre, and everything else was sort of, off of that, what would it be?

CAROL: What?

EDDIE: When is the weather real, and at home, and not just a version of the weather? What month is actually England?

CAROL: I don't know.

EDDIE: I think like, or what about the seasons? Which of the seasons is like, actually what England is really like?

CAROL: Well. I suppose. Autumn.

EDDIE: That's what I think. And about getting dark.

CAROL: What?

EDDIE: I think it's normal time for getting dark in October. And everything looks right in October. That's when it's like – this is England, you know?

CAROL: You're so odd, you know that?

EDDIE: Finish this off shall we?

CAROL: If you'd like to.

EDDIE: Course I'd like to, Carol.

CAROL: I shouldn't really. I've got so much work to do tomorrow, can't believe it.

EDDIE: Yeah?

CAROL: We had a computer malfunction today, data malfunction. Trying to – well it doesn't matter what we were trying to do, I can't talk about it. Makes me feel sick to think about it. And today, I get so stressed, I went into the IT department to sort things out, and there was no one there to help me, they were all on lunch or something, and I just cried. Isn't that terrible?

EDDIE: Oh, Carol.

CAROL: I know. I think I've been under stress.

EDDIE: You shouldn't be letting yourself get stressed. It's not worth it. Nothing's worth it really, is it.

CAROL: I know, I know.

EDDIE: Shall I be mother?

CAROL: You go ahead.

He pours their drinks, hands one to CAROL.

EDDIE: You all right?

CAROL: I was just thinking how strange it is we're together here really.

EDDIE: I know what you mean.

CAROL: You never know what's going to happen to you, do you.

EDDIE gets up and moves to sit on the floor.

EDDIE: I know.

CAROL: You all right?

EDDIE: I like looking at you.

CAROL: Oh.

EDDIE: It's easier to talk when you're looking at someone than when you're sitting next to them, I think. They shouldn't do that to you. It's terrible. Getting you so stressed.

CAROL: Well. Lots of people have it worse than me.

EDDIE: All the same.

CAROL: I've got a good job and I must remember to stay glad of that, even on the bad days, you know. This tastes better the more you drink it, doesn't it.

EDDIE: Yeah.

CAROL: How like life.

CAROL laughs.

EDDIE: What are you laughing at?

CAROL: Oh, sorry, it's just a joke we have in the office. Little joke. 'How like life.' We say that about things and it makes us laugh. You know. Someone says at a meeting, we've had an exceptionally low turnout at this election. And Wendy says, or I say, or whoever, 'how like life'. It's making fun, see.

EDDIE: Out of what?

CAROL: Well I don't know, really. People who are sincere. You know, all that inspirational messages – stuff. You don't have to keep calm and carry on to work here but it helps.

EDDIE: I don't have a clue what you're talking about.

CAROL: No, you wouldn't, you don't have to work in an office.

EDDIE: I'm sure it's funny though.

CAROL: Yes, thank you, I'm aware that it's not. Just makes us laugh. I get shy I think, when I'm on my own with people.

EDDIE: Or is it just me?

CAROL: I don't know. I'm not often on my own with anyone like this. Makes me feel a bit frightened.

EDDIE: Why?

CAROL: I don't know. Maybe I feel like I don't know what's going to happen. It's just not being used to things, that's all it is. Sorry, I'm talking too much. I'm feeling very tired. You know sometimes I get very very tired. I think perhaps I'm going to go to bed.

EDDIE: Are you?

CAROL: I think I'm tired enough to sleep, yeah.

EDDIE: Come on then.

EDDIE gets up.

CAROL: What?

EDDIE: Big hug.

CAROL: Big hug?

EDDIE: Come here.

CAROL: Eddie.

EDDIE: There we go. Big hug. Let's have a little dance, come on.

CAROL: You're so silly.

EDDIE: Doo be doo be doo, be doo be doo, be doo be doo.

CAROL: Eddie.

EDDIE: What? Made you smile, didn't I? And you were getting all mardy, weren't you.

CAROL: You're so silly.

EDDIE: Thank you for this, Carol. I really mean it. I'm so grateful.

CAROL: It's my pleasure, really.

EDDIE: What you smiling like that for?

CAROL: Just you. You look better than you did this afternoon, shivering there on that bench. I'm so glad to see you looking well, Eddie.

EDDIE: Thanks.

CAROL: I'm so pleased this has happened.

EDDIE: Yeah?

CAROL: I'm so pleased to have had the chance to – well, anyway.

EDDIE and CAROL look at each other, then laugh.

CAROL: It's all right though. It's all right.

EDDIE: Yeah? Make it sound sort of serious.

CAROL: Maybe it is.

EDDIE: Yeah?

CAROL: Well you might have been the most serious I ever felt about anyone. Nice to swim in this sea again, you know?

EDDIE: Yeah. It is, yeah.

CAROL: Well.

EDDIE: You okay?

CAROL: Fine. Sore back today.

EDDIE: Yeah?

CAROL: That's getting old.

EDDIE: You're not old.

CAROL: No. Thank you for noticing. I'd better –

EDDIE: Sure you're all right?

CAROL: Totally. Don't worry. Just tired.

EDDIE: Night then Carol.

CAROL: Night night.

Exit CAROL. EDDIE sits back down on the sofa and finishes his drink, then pours himself another.

2

The sitting room. The bedding has disappeared. EDDIE has several carrier bags of paperwork with him.

CAROL: These are your things?

EDDIE: Yeah.

CAROL: This is how you keep it all?

EDDIE: It's sort of waterproof.

CAROL: I don't really know if it is, love.

EDDIE: Isn't it?

CAROL: Well, no. They're not sealed, are they, carrier bags.

EDDIE: It's all I had, Carol.

CAROL: I understand. Let me just get my shoes off, do you mind?

EDDIE: Sorry.

CAROL starts taking off her shoes.

EDDIE: I should have said yes to a key, shouldn't I.

CAROL: Waiting out there in the rain. Will you take a key now?

EDDIE: All right. Thank you.

CAROL: Completely fine. Not very warm today, is it.

EDDIE: Not very.

CAROL: Let me just –

CAROL leans over the sofa and chucks her shoes in the direction of the door.

There we go. Right. What are we doing with all this then?

EDDIE: Well I thought maybe I'd just get rid of it all.

CAROL: Really?

EDDIE: Clean slate. Start again. Fresh start.

CAROL: You've just carted it all the way over here, you sure you want to throw it out?

EDDIE: I can't think of anything that matters to me in here.

CAROL: No? All right.

EDDIE: Maybe you'd help me go through it all though, before I chuck it away or whatever?

CAROL: Yeah, okay.

EDDIE: Just in case. Just in case I've forgotten about something important.

CAROL: What sort of thing?

EDDIE: I don't know. Something I might want to keep.

CAROL: All right. All right, let's do that then. Give me one of those.

EDDIE: Do you mind which one?

CAROL: Whatever you think's best, Eddie.

EDDIE: Just this one, maybe.

CAROL: Great. Do you want a cup of tea before we start?

EDDIE: I'm all right.

CAROL: All right. I might sit here, I think.

CAROL sits down on the sofa. EDDIE sits down on the floor.

CAROL: How do you want to go through it?

EDDIE: Maybe let's do essential paperwork, and non-essential paperwork, sort of thing.

CAROL: How do we know which is which?

EDDIE: We decide.

CAROL: Is any of this gonna be actually essential, do you think?

EDDIE: I haven't looked at it in so long, I couldn't tell you.

CAROL: Yeah. Well let's make a start and see, shall we?

She empties the bag out on the sofa and looks through it.

CAROL: This is old letters.

EDDIE: Who from?

CAROL: Might have to be you works that out, Eddie.

EDDIE: Course, sorry.

CAROL: There you go.

CAROL hands EDDIE a letter. He scrutinises it.

EDDIE: I can't read the writing. Look at that. Like a child did it.

CAROL: So we chuck that do we?

EDDIE: Why?

CAROL: If we can't even read them.

EDDIE: But if we could read them then what would they say?

CAROL: Fair point. Maybe I'll pile up letters here and we can decide about them later.

EDDIE: Yeah. Cool. Yeah.

CAROL: I'm pretty sure that most of this is bank statements.

EDDIE: Right.

CAROL: I think they're for banks in other countries, actually, look at that, funny logo. Isn't that pretty?

EDDIE: I wouldn't know how to get into that now. I don't think there's any money in it though, it's okay, I emptied everything.

CAROL: Great.

EDDIE: So let's make a deal that anything dating more than seven years ago from the bank can go in the bin.

CAROL: Seven years?

EDDIE: In case I get audited.

CAROL: I don't know whether you need to worry about having your old Nigerian bank accounts audited, Eddie, I don't know who's going to do that. If HMRC get hold of you they'll have quite enough to worry about already.

EDDIE: So we should chuck away everything from the bank?

CAROL: I think we might as well, yeah.

EDDIE: Right. Fuck. I'm sorry. I'm finding this a bit difficult, Carol.

CAROL: I can tell.

EDDIE: It actually is very hard to throw any of this away because what if no one remembers me any more one day? You know?

CAROL: It's all right, Eddie.

EDDIE: I know. Sorry. I'm being stupid. Let's do what you say.

CAROL: Yeah?

EDDIE: Everything from Nigeria or – that's Norway, I think – in the bin pile.

CAROL: All right.

EDDIE: Where shall we put the bin pile?

CAROL: What about here?

EDDIE: Yeah. Then we can both reach it.

CAROL: Exactly.

EDDIE: I'll have a look in here. See if there's other countries.

They take a bag each, and sort it, binning old bank statements. The dialogue runs over this action.

EDDIE: Maybe we can keep the letters.

CAROL: It's all right, we can keep the letters.

EDDIE: I don't wanna take up too much space.

CAROL: You won't be taking up space, it's fine.

EDDIE: I just don't want to get rid of them in case one day I remember who they came from, in case I kept them because they were important.

CAROL: Absolutely. I understand.

EDDIE stops and looks at the bin pile. It takes CAROL a moment to notice.

CAROL: What's up, love? You all right?

EDDIE: I've been alive for so long and I haven't got anything to show for it.

CAROL: You have, Eddie. You have. In your head, you've. Just not in possessions terms, that's all.

EDDIE: I used to think I didn't want to have things. I didn't want to care about things. I didn't really want to care about anything. It's only a way of getting yourself down, innit. Look at this. I haven't got anything to show for it all.

CAROL: It's okay.

EDDIE: You've got all this.

CAROL: All what?

EDDIE: I dunno. Nice house.

CAROL: Oh, you don't wanna envy people their houses.
They're a burden as much as they're anything else.

EDDIE: D'you think?

CAROL: Imagine all the time you haven't wasted worrying
about your mortgage.

EDDIE: You said you hadn't got a mortgage.

CAROL: No, but some people.

EDDIE: True.

CAROL: And they make you a target for burglaries, houses. No
one ever burgled a tent.

EDDIE: People set fire to tents.

CAROL: And people set fire to houses, we're prey to that as
well. Feral youth. There was a terrible story in the news the
other week about a man with learning difficulties, who was
actually on the register, but no one knew that at first, who
got sort of turned into a house slave by these boys. They
moved into his house and made him, I don't know, they
weren't very nice to him, they just played their Playstations
or whatever. And then when they found out he was a sex
offender they killed him.

EDDIE: Right.

CAROL: Quite horribly, but we don't need to talk about that.

EDDIE: Right.

CAROL: But the terrible thing was the live links though. You
know on the news on your computer, they have different
live links that take you through to the related stories?

EDDIE: Right.

CAROL: Well I clicked on one. And it was a court report from
a few years earlier that was really very similar, except this

time the poor man who died hadn't been a sex offender at all.

EDDIE: Even worse then.

CAROL: And then I clicked on a live link on that page, and it took me to a very similar story from a few years earlier, except this time the learning difficulties person had been a woman, and she was an American.

EDDIE: Right.

CAROL: And I started to get so panicked. Because it was all over the world, you see. You start to realise it's happening everywhere, people are doing it to each other everywhere, there are loads of stories like this. And then I read a story about a girl who got set on fire and left in a wood and I just had to shut the page I was so upset, you know?

EDDIE: I'm sorry you got so upset.

CAROL: Well.

EDDIE: They say that about Fritzl and whatever.

CAROL: What do they say?

EDDIE: There's loads of people doing what he did. We only ever hear about the thickos.

CAROL: Learning difficulties, Eddie, you don't say thickos now.

EDDIE: Sorry.

CAROL: I don't know how there could be very many men who want a woman in their basement. It would actually be very difficult, I think. Take a lot of ingenuity. You could never have anyone round.

EDDIE: I think the world's full of people who never have anyone round.

CAROL: Well. They must be very lonely.

EDDIE: Perhaps that's why they get a woman in the basement.

CAROL: Yeah, maybe there comes a point when it seems like a good idea. I don't know why we're talking about this, it's quite disturbing.

EDDIE: Sorry.

CAROL: I think it was me who started it. I talked about the learning difficulties sex offender didn't I. I knew I was going to. Sometimes I get a thing trapped in my head and it's circling and circling and I know it's going to come out some time. And I've been on my own so much, I can never tell any more how things are going to sound when I say them to another person. I do think it's a good thing, having this house.

EDDIE: Yeah?

CAROL: Something solid. I don't want to sound like I'm not grateful for what I've had. Helps you know where you are.

EDDIE: Yeah.

CAROL: This place hasn't changed since we first moved in, you know. I've had the same landscape all my life.

EDDIE: All the time you've lived here?

CAROL: All my life nearly, yeah. Mum and Dad did a bang up job when we came here, that was the last big change.

EDDIE: Did you never want to redecorate?

CAROL: No, I redecorate. Keep doing it up when it's needed. But it's more about sprucing than changing. I just keep it all looking good. And obviously Leanne helps out as well.

EDDIE: Right.

CAROL: Anyway. Two bags done.

EDDIE: Yeah.

CAROL: Made a start. That's a good bit of work isn't it.

EDDIE: I might need your help with something else as well, actually.

CAROL: Oh right?

EDDIE: I went to my GP this morning.

CAROL: Oh, okay. Have you been struggling?

EDDIE: Well, you know. It's always a struggle really.

CAROL: Yeah.

EDDIE: I came back partly cos I thought the NHS, you know.

CAROL: Of course.

EDDIE: So I've been looking for help, yeah. I feel like I need a bit of help.

CAROL: But things aren't set up for you just yet?

EDDIE: It's slow, man. You earn whatever you get from that lot, I tell you.

CAROL: What's holding things up?

EDDIE: A lot of things are difficult. It's hard to talk about, you know?

CAROL: Of course.

EDDIE: The GP I'm with, when I registered, I was getting all my post sent to a friend, right. Now she and I aren't talking. So that's sort of difficult. Cos even if there are referral letters coming, it takes a while for me to see them. Cos she won't answer my calls.

CAROL: Why don't you change your postal address to here?

EDDIE: Yeah. Maybe, yeah. Would you mind?

CAROL: Course not, if it helped. Call the GP and get it changed and then you'll be quicker getting everything sorted.

EDDIE: It's all so fiddly.

CAROL: I know.

EDDIE: Everything about it's complicated, it's all getting blood out a stone. You tell them you're ill but if you're not gonna cut yourself you're not really ill enough for them to help you.

CAROL: I know that's how it can feel.

EDDIE: No, that's what they said to me. The quickest way to get seen is if I try and kill myself. It's a shame really, cos there was an. Attempt. But that was back in Nigeria so I don't think it'd count, I don't think it'd bump me up the list if I told them, and it gave me a bad fucking head ache and I'm in a better place now, don't wanna try it again just for attention.

CAROL: An attempt?

EDDIE: Sort of hosepipe in the window sort of thing.

CAROL: Oh, no.

EDDIE: Believe me man, the headache you get off the fumes, I fucking hated it.

CAROL: That why you didn't go through with it?

EDDIE: No. I was found.

CAROL: God, Eddie.

EDDIE: Yeah. That was the other reason I left there, I guess.

CAROL: I'm so sorry.

EDDIE: I don't think it was your fault.

CAROL: No. I'm just expressing sympathy. I'm sorry that happened to you.

EDDIE: Oh, yeah.

CAROL: You don't think you'll try it again, you feel a bit better?

EDDIE: I do, yeah. I'm fine. I'm just a bit on my own, you know?

CAROL: Yeah.

EDDIE: I think I'm the only black man in Havant.

CAROL: No.

EDDIE: Not enough of us for a football team anyway.

CAROL: No.

EDDIE: Sometimes I don't feel much less foreign here than I ever have done anywhere else. But that's all right, maybe, I know where I am on my own.

CAROL: You always quite liked that feeling.

EDDIE: Yeah, you know me Carol, don't you.

CAROL: Maybe I do.

EDDIE: I've thought of you a lot, you know.

CAROL: Yeah?

EDDIE: Wondered if I'd bump into you again somehow. Can I tell you something?

CAROL: Go on.

EDDIE: Nah, I'd better not.

CAROL: What?

EDDIE: No, no, mistake, sorry. Forget it. Anyway, what I was saying. I have to fill out a form to get the counselling. I was wondering if you could help.

CAROL: Oh. Okay.

EDDIE: Just I try to think about what to say, and I get sort of emotional, and I can't keep my mind on it.

CAROL: All right. You want to do that now then?

EDDIE: We can't now.

CAROL: Okay.

EDDIE: Form got ruined in the rain. I'll go back tomorrow and pick up a new one.

CAROL: Great.

EDDIE: Thank you.

CAROL: It's completely fine, Eddie, completely.

EDDIE starts tidying away the papers.

CAROL: Always used to push help away really, didn't you.

EDDIE: All my life.

CAROL: I ever caught you looking glum I'd ask what was up and you'd tell me a joke. You always knew so many jokes. I used to be so frightened of how easy you found everything.

EDDIE: I never thought anything was, you know.

CAROL: Really?

EDDIE: Just wanted people to think I was all right. Nothing's ever been fine. I just wanted people to think I was all right so I didn't have to talk to anyone, so I could just stay out of everything.

CAROL: Yeah.

EDDIE: Trouble is that's all very nice when you're young, but look at me. I'll never last at anything normal now, will I. I don't know. Maybe there's a reason the world works like it does, and people live how they live. Maybe it's not so small to be ordinary, in the long run, when you start to get older and think about your savings. I always felt – never liked what I had, you know?

CAROL: Even though you had so much going for you.

EDDIE: I know, that wasn't the problem. I just felt so crowded here.

CAROL: By what?

EDDIE: I dunno. I can't really say. People's troubles, you know? And they get you into bother, and you never really get over anything that happens.

CAROL: Oh, that's true.

EDDIE: Yeah.

CAROL: I remember when we came back here, after Ray left. How strange it was. Because you think to yourself, we're getting back to something, we're getting on with it, we'll pick it all up again. But it's five years later, that's the thing. You're not getting back to anything, your life's been going on, it's happening, and you've done whatever with it, you have however long left. It made me very frightened, it was a frightening time.

EDDIE: Yeah.

CAROL: Sometimes I think my whole life has been a frightening time. Well. I remember the crunch of the gravel under my feet walking back up the drive, and thinking my life might be over. I might have had all of my fun. But I was wrong, it turned out. I've had a lot of good things since. And of course I have Leanne. You never know what there is coming.

EDDIE: Leanne never calls you, does she.

CAROL: Oh, yeah, she does.

EDDIE: Oh?

CAROL: She just calls at funny times.

EDDIE: Oh right.

CAROL: Calls me at work most of the time.

EDDIE: Oh yeah.

CAROL: And she's so busy as well, all she's got going on, it has to be funny times.

EDDIE: You ought to make sure you hang out with her, Carol. Cos it's all slipping past us. You want to grab it while you can. Your own little armful of life.

CAROL: Right.

EDDIE: When I was a kid and I was growing up, I didn't live with my parents. I was fostered. Did you know that?

CAROL: Yeah, you told me that before.

EDDIE: That's how I ended up in Portsmouth. Cath and Nigel Owen, those were their names, my foster parents. They didn't mean any harm, of course.

CAROL: Yeah.

EDDIE: I lived in this white house, white parents, foster brothers, sisters coming and going, till I moved out and started my life. I used to lie awake and think about my parents, my real parents, my mum and dad. That was how I learned it. You get so little of anything. And that wasn't just my mum and dad, it was everything. All gone almost before it's happened to you. Then it's back in the dark again, and racist schoolkids, and crying and lonely all the time.

CAROL: What happened to your parents?

EDDIE: My dad died, and my mum remarried, and my step dad already had a family, and there wasn't room.

CAROL: I'm sorry.

EDDIE: Yeah. Fucking hell.

CAROL: What?

EDDIE: No, no, nothing. I'm okay. Can I tell you a story?

CAROL: All right.

EDDIE: There was a ship once called the Flying Dutchman. In the old days, a sailing ship, Blackbeard, you know. And this ship was cursed. The captain of the ship was doomed to wander the ocean, and only set foot on dry land for one night every seven years. He'd done something, I don't know what he'd done. And he could only break the curse if on that one night, he got someone to fall in love with him. Not sleep with him, I mean actually fall in love. Isn't that amazing?

CAROL: Why?

EDDIE: It's about us.

CAROL: I'm not cursed, Eddie.

EDDIE: Not like that. I mean it's what it's like, isn't it. Think about it. Trying to make land. It's about us.

CAROL: Right.

EDDIE: You don't get it.

CAROL: I don't know.

EDDIE: Think about it. You might get it.

CAROL: What's the rest of the story?

EDDIE: What d'you mean?

CAROL: That's just the setup. What happens, how does it end?

EDDIE: Oh. Well. Someone falls in love with him, and he gets to go home.

3

CAROL has a form and a pen. EDDIE is standing, agitated.

CAROL: Has someone been here today?

EDDIE: How d'you mean?

CAROL: There's just a smell in the air, there's a perfume. Have you had someone round?

EDDIE: I got a new deodorant.

CAROL: That must be it.

EDDIE: Yeah.

CAROL: Important to smell nice.

EDDIE: Do you think I don't?

CAROL: I didn't mean that. Come on, let's do this now. What do you want to say?

EDDIE: Well. I wanna say that I don't see the point of anything. So I can't find the energy for anything. Because every time I start to do something, I remember that in a little while I'm going to be dead, and I won't exist any more. Because there isn't a heaven or a hell, I don't think, is there. I don't see how there can be. I think that's just a swizz. I wish it wasn't, I really do. Where did I get to?

CAROL: I'm not writing it down yet, I just wanna listen and get a sense of the whole thing we're gonna put in this box, you know?

EDDIE: Yeah, good idea yeah.

CAROL: So we want to say you don't see the point in anything, because you feel like whatever you do you're gonna die, is that it?

EDDIE: Yeah. No matter how much I care about anything now, I'm still gonna end up dead, so why should I care about anything? And it's worse than that. Anything I've ever cared about till now in my life has already died. Every project I ever had has failed. Every friendship I ever had has gone. I've already lived to see all the things I ever cared about end, already, and that's only like, I dunno like halfway through the road I'm meant to be walking, so how am I supposed to feel like I could put my back into anything again? If everything's already gone to shit and I've hardly even started?

CAROL: Yeah.

EDDIE: Except you're here of course. You're here, and that's not nothing. I have got that.

CAROL: Yeah. So we want to say that you don't see how to hope for anything?

EDDIE: I see no escape.

CAROL: From what?

EDDIE: Dunno. I see no escape.

CAROL: Okay.

EDDIE: I want to show someone just once how fucking vast it is, being here. Even if it looks so stupid and so small, my life, you know. If someone would only just see. I want my life to have a meaning. And it seems so obvious to me that it can't. Because it's not like that, is it. It's just one foot in front of the other till you're dead.

CAROL: Yeah.

EDDIE: So if we put that, that'll do it.

CAROL: Okay. So what if I put something like, I see no hope for anything and that's really hard because I don't know how not to hope for things, even though I know there's no point, and I don't know how to care about anything when I know I'll be dead anyway before very long, and everything I've ever done has failed and life just feels so pointless, if we say something like that?

EDDIE: Yeah. That's what I said.

CAROL: Should we put something about the background to the situation?

EDDIE: Like all the past and whatever?

CAROL: That sort of thing.

EDDIE: Yeah, yeah we should. Then they'll know it's serious. I worry they'll think that I'm making it up.

CAROL: No one will think you're making it up. What shall we say about things that have happened before then?

EDDIE: Well. We ought to say I grew up in England but I had to leave because I had a mental breakdown.

CAROL: Is that what it was?

EDDIE: What do you think it was?

CAROL: I don't know. All I knew was that you disappeared one day, you never told me you were going. I never saw you to find anything out, did I.

EDDIE: No. I couldn't. I had to get away.

CAROL: Okay.

EDDIE: I'm sorry I did that to you.

CAROL: It doesn't matter. What else shall we say?

EDDIE: Well I got out of England. And then I didn't know what to do for a while. Cos I never – you know I had this feeling I'd got lost somewhere. Like there'd been a Plan A, but I couldn't remember it. And till I worked it out, I couldn't do anything. So I was just trying to – there was nothing I wanted to do for a long time. And I started to feel like it must be because I didn't know myself, you know, I didn't know who I was. Like, there must have been a stream running somewhere, that was me, and if I could just find it I could drink it, and then I'd know what to do with my life. But I didn't know where it was. So I kind of – well I went to Nigeria, didn't I.

CAROL: Yeah.

EDDIE: I thought if I went to Nigeria maybe I'd find myself. And it was pretty easy to get work there. Lot of drilling going on. Big Chinese companies. But there aren't any Nigerians do those engineering jobs, they get the cleaning jobs, the skilled work gets shipped in. So I didn't really meet any Nigerians, I worked with Norwegians, or whatever. I ended up feeling like a foreigner, really.

CAROL: Well you were, weren't you.

EDDIE: Yeah, that was the thing, yeah. So anyway, I did some of that. And a lot of work all over like that. Or other work, or. And I ended up a lot of places. And then one day I lost a job, and I went for a walk, and I realised it had been eighteen years since I'd been in England.

CAROL: So you came home.

EDDIE: Well, Havant was never home for me.

CAROL: Course, you were Portsmouth, weren't you.

EDDIE: Yeah, so I went back to Portsmouth first. We go home, don't we. When we need to lick our wounds. I didn't want to work on rigs or whatever any more, I was feeling quite dark when I got here really, didn't want to work at all, but I had a bit of money so I lived off that, then I needed some more so I looked for work, and I ended up here.

CAROL: Okay. And then you were living in the tent.

EDDIE: No, that was only recent.

CAROL: Oh right.

EDDIE: I had this mobile library van for a bit. Cosy. I parked it in car parks. But it blew up.

CAROL: Blew up?

EDDIE: Yeah. Normal morning. I put the key in the ignition, big fire started behind me. Three fire engines.

CAROL: Really?

EDDIE: I had a gas canister in the back to do the cooking, they thought it might go. Inside, right, inside, it was all plastic moulding, you know, the interior, and after the fire it had all melted. Looked amazing. Like the waxwork zombie things in horror movies. You know, melted faces.

CAROL: Melted faces.

EDDIE: Or that Salvador Dali clock, you know?

CAROL: Right.

EDDIE: So we'll put in some of that. And then put in the tent. And say you're looking after me but it can't last for ever and I need some proper help.

CAROL: I'm not gonna kick you out Eddie, don't worry.

EDDIE: Yeah, but I can't stay here for ever. And I have heard that before, you know. No offence, but I've heard it before from people.

CAROL: What?

EDDIE: People have told me I won't have to go before now. I've always ended up back in the tent.

CAROL: I'm sorry.

EDDIE: Well. We had some fun back in the old days, didn't we?

CAROL: Yeah.

EDDIE: Good times.

CAROL: Yeah.

EDDIE: I've always had you as a happy memory, cos we had some good times. I never went wandering cos it was what I wanted. No animal ever went anywhere it didn't have to, that's what they tell you in zoos, that's why they say it's all right that they're caged up so small. I would have liked a life in one place. It never works. Always burns me. Anyone I ever trust, they go, they send me away. It's the minute it starts to feel good then it's over.

CAROL: Are you saying that because you think there's stuff going wrong between you and me?

EDDIE: No. I'm just scared.

CAROL: Why?

EDDIE: Because I'm happy here with you. And when I feel happy I know what's coming next.

CAROL: Eddie, I think someone has been here.

EDDIE: Oh?

CAROL: There's lipstick on that mug, I don't wear lipstick.

EDDIE: Checking up on me now then?

CAROL: Not really, Eddie, you just haven't done the washing up.

EDDIE: I didn't know it always had to be done straight away.

CAROL: Has someone been round then?

EDDIE: Yeah, I had a visitor, yeah.

CAROL: Okay.

EDDIE: Sorry.

CAROL: Can I ask who it was?

EDDIE: Well it was actually my ex. You know I told you about my friend I was living with?

CAROL: Yeah.

EDDIE: It was actually her.

CAROL: Did the two of you just need to have a talk, or –

EDDIE: That's it.

CAROL: You didn't want to meet in public.

EDDIE: We needed to talk a few things over.

CAROL: Right.

EDDIE: I'm sorry, I should have asked. I didn't mean to disrespect you. I have massive respect for you Carol, I'm sorry. You know what I'm like.

CAROL: I'm gonna make some tea, all right?

EDDIE: Okay.

CAROL: Will you have one?

EDDIE: Yeah, thanks.

CAROL: All right.

4

Evening. CAROL is sitting on the sofa reading. Enter EDDIE.

EDDIE: All right?

CAROL: Hello.

EDDIE: Okay?

CAROL: Yeah. You all right?

EDDIE: Not really.

CAROL: You eaten?

EDDIE: Had a kebab.

CAROL: Eddie.

EDDIE: It was easy.

CAROL: Might as well slap it straight on your thighs. Have you been drinking?

EDDIE: A bit.

CAROL: I've got some news.

EDDIE: Oh yeah?

CAROL: Good news, hopefully.

41

EDDIE: Go on.

CAROL: Your letter came.

EDDIE: Yeah?

CAROL: So that's positive, isn't it. Good things come to those who wait.

EDDIE: Unless they gas themselves in the mean time.

CAROL: Eddie.

EDDIE: Sorry.

CAROL: Not even in jest.

EDDIE: Sorry. Where is it?

CAROL: Here you go.

EDDIE: Thanks.

EDDIE sits down with the letter as CAROL hands it to him.

EDDIE: Feel really nervous.

CAROL: You mustn't pin your hopes on it too much, of course. It's not gonna make you feel better overnight.

EDDIE: I know.

CAROL: You only get better yourself in the end, don't you, really. Let's see what it says then.

EDDIE: I sort of don't want to.

CAROL: Why not?

EDDIE: If it says no.

CAROL: If they say no then we just look at the next option. If they say no then it'll be all right.

EDDIE: They can't say no till I open it though. So I don't wanna open it.

CAROL: But you can't do that for ever.

EDDIE: I just feel on my own. I don't wanna feel worse when I open it.

CAROL: I know.

EDDIE: I know you're helping but I feel on my own.

CAROL: It's all right. I know.

EDDIE opens the letter. He takes out a leaflet and a letter. He reads.

EDDIE: Well fuck that then.

CAROL: Oh, no.

EDDIE: I don't meet the criteria.

CAROL: Do they say anything else?

EDDIE: There's a leaflet. Can you look at it? I don't wanna look at it.

He hands CAROL the leaflet and the letter.

CAROL: Are you feeling low? You may find the enclosed leaflet helpful.

EDDIE: Well that's something to look forward to, isn't it.

CAROL: Right. Cup of tea?

EDDIE: Yes please.

CAROL: Okay.

CAROL exits. EDDIE sits in silence. CAROL comes back in again.

CAROL: It'll be a minute.

EDDIE: Yeah.

CAROL: I'm really sorry they haven't offered you more, Eddie.

EDDIE: Yeah. Ah well. Sucks, but it is what it is though, innit.

CAROL: Just have to keep on, won't you.

EDDIE: Yeah.

CAROL: Are you feeling okay?

EDDIE: I don't know. Not really. I don't think I have a choice about it.

CAROL: No, I suppose you don't.

EDDIE: I suppose I have to be all right.

CAROL: Yeah.

EDDIE: All right. I'll be all right then. Let's talk about something else. How was your day?

CAROL: Oh, fine, thanks for asking.

EDDIE: Do anything fun?

CAROL: Not much. Went to work. Came home. Had some dinner. That's about it really. What about you?

EDDIE: I don't know. I don't know how to do anything now.

CAROL: It's all right.

EDDIE: I just don't know how to get out of the feeling I'm in. I don't know what I'm gonna do.

CAROL: No.

EDDIE: You might even be right about the rewilding.

CAROL: Yeah?

EDDIE: I might not have thought it through. I think I need a project though, you know?

CAROL: Everyone needs a hobby.

EDDIE: More than that, a life, we all need a life, I think. I was thinking about it. I thought I might like to be a teaching assistant. Or nursery school or something.

CAROL: Yeah?

EDDIE: I liked school. You could think someone was in charge still. And it wasn't all. And it was still all off in the future.

CAROL: Yeah.

EDDIE: Nothing's set up and waiting for us at all, actually. No one's organised anything, you have to do all of it yourself. I'd like to be back in a school again.

CAROL: That might be a good idea.

EDDIE: I don't know. Maybe I need to just stay where I am one time. It's not so terrible, dredging for scrap. It's so terrifying that you don't get what you want. What I really wish, I wish there was some kind of system where they worked out at the start of your life how much money you were going to earn, and gave it to you up front. I'd still go into work. It'd just be so much better to know that the money was there.

CAROL: Yeah, but then what if you only got a tiny bit? And then you had to live like that.

EDDIE: I spose. I think I have to probably accept that I'm not going to have some idea that's going to make me rich. I should accept that isn't going to happen. Because it would have happened by now. I was thinking what I need to do is find somewhere I want to live, and find some work I can do there. That's maybe what I'll work on next.

CAROL: Like where?

EDDIE: I dunno. Lyme Regis or something. I like Lyme Regis. Went there once for a holiday. There's a dinosaur museum, isn't there.

CAROL: Fossil museum, I think.

EDDIE: Same thing.

CAROL: So you want to move to Lyme Regis.

EDDIE: I don't know. Just, anywhere but here. I can't believe this is my one and only life, and the whole world exists, and I've spent fucking half of it in Portsmouth, you know?

CAROL: Yeah?

EDDIE: I dunno. You're born where you're born in the end, aren't you. You always liked it here.

CAROL: It's all right.

EDDIE: You must have been lonely before I got here.

CAROL: Well –

EDDIE: Did you never want to get away from this place?

CAROL: Why?

EDDIE: Don't you think you could be doing more?

CAROL: More what?

EDDIE: I don't know. I just think if you're alive in the world, and you're living in Havant, that's quite a choice you're making. You know? You can live in the Alps, Tuscany, Outer Mongolia. You're here.

CAROL: People are happy here.

EDDIE: People value different things to me. I've never been very good at understanding things that weren't me, really. That's part of my problem. So people who want. Family and security and community and routine. I don't know about them.

CAROL: You don't know about me, you mean.

EDDIE: Maybe I don't. I feel like I do though. Feel like I know something important about you. And where you're from. When I saw you in the park the other week. I don't know. It was like the whole last twenty years of my life didn't have to have vanished. Because you were still here. Sometimes it's like time isn't passing at all, up here. It was like I might be able to walk straight back into the past.

CAROL: I felt the same.

EDDIE: Did you really never fancy it? Just packing up and going somewhere else, going away from here?

CAROL: No, I'm hefted, me.

EDDIE: You what?

CAROL: It's a thing with sheep. A hefted sheep is one that finds its way back to its home acre if you move it away. That's me, I'm hefted, I've got my home.

EDDIE: And what a lovely home it is too.

CAROL: Well it's all right, isn't it. I did move away for a little bit, mind. To Hayling.

EDDIE: Yeah?

CAROL: Didn't last, it was a mistake really.

EDDIE: I thought Hayling was nice.

CAROL: Oh yeah, it's lovely. Home of the holiday camp. All started there, after the war. Some of Billy Butlin's cousins still run the fairground, and he was from there, you know. It's like that, that world, they all seem to intermarry, don't they. Not inbreeding, just – family. But the last bus back from Havant's ten to ten. Ten to five on a Sunday. And I was always round to Mum's because she babysat, so it was silly. Moved back after a year.

EDDIE: That's where Leanne is now though, isn't it.

CAROL: Yeah, she likes it. It's a free room, on the site, and you're more part of it if you stay, you know?

EDDIE: Perhaps it wasn't such a bad thing you took her to Hayling, then. Perhaps she'd thank you for it.

CAROL: I'd never really thought of that. Isn't that a nice thought? Thank you, that's a really nice thought. I don't think she likes it here so much.

EDDIE: No?

CAROL: Well. It's a very empty place now. And we haven't got anywhere good to eat, what I call a voucher code

47

restaurant. Not like Portsmouth. You know Portsmouth's very good now.

EDDIE: Really?

CAROL: Award-winning car park.

EDDIE: That's nice. I didn't know there was a car park Oscars.

CAROL: There's all sorts of things you'd never think would exist around, aren't there.

EDDIE: Yeah.

CAROL: People set like concrete don't they. You know they say you shouldn't make faces? Or the wind'll change and it'll stick. That's how I feel, really.

EDDIE: Don't say that, Carol.

CAROL: It's just how I feel.

EDDIE: I'm sorry.

CAROL: Nothing to be done I don't think, nothing for it.

EDDIE: When did you come here, when you were a baby?

CAROL: We grew up in Leigh Park after they built it. Before it was bad, you know. We moved over here when it was starting to get all rough, my dad's job meant we could buy somewhere. Lucky, you know?

EDDIE: What did your dad do?

CAROL: He had a shop. I don't remember much about it. Hardware. Buckets. I couldn't tell you much else. He died when I was quite young, so.

EDDIE: Really?

CAROL: Yeah, when I was eight.

EDDIE: I didn't know that. Did your mum ever marry anyone else?

CAROL: Well, you know. He was her husband.

EDDIE: Yeah. I didn't know that about you.

CAROL: Yeah.

EDDIE: What's wrong Carol?

CAROL: I'm sorry. Oh, silly. It's funny how things take you by surprise. I was just thinking it's sad Mum never had anyone else. I hope she was happy, she was a long time on her own, I never think of it really.

EDDIE goes to her, holds her.

EDDIE: It's all right. You're all right.

He tries to kiss her. CAROL kisses him back. Then she stops.

CAROL: I can't do that.

EDDIE: It's all right.

CAROL: I'm sorry, will you get off me please? Get off me.

EDDIE: All right. I'm sorry. I didn't mean to do the wrong thing.

CAROL: We're just both feeling vulnerable, aren't we. We're just both feeling knocked off our feet.

EDDIE: Why don't you want to?

CAROL: I can't.

EDDIE: Why not? We're here, aren't we, we're together.

CAROL: I'm walled in. I'd like to get out but I can't, I'm sorry. I don't know how not to be frightened of someone any more.

EDDIE: Okay. I'm sorry.

CAROL: It's so frightening being alive isn't it, because you get to go on all of the rides just once. I think I've done this one. I think it's finished, I don't think I get to do it again.

That's what it feels like. People's lives get mapped out once they're far enough into them, don't they. I don't think this will come again. I'd rather not risk myself around these kinds of feelings. This is all twenty years ago for me, I can't go back, I can't do it.

EDDIE: I didn't mean to do the wrong thing.

CAROL: I know.

EDDIE: You never said that I mattered to you. Back then. I thought I was just someone you were seeing. I didn't know you wanted any more.

CAROL: Neither did I. I didn't know you were important then. That's hindsight's done that. I didn't know what my life was going to be about. I thought there might have been others. You know, people at work used to ask me whether I'd ever got over Ray. Not for a long time now, no one ever asks me about Ray any more. And I'd ask them, did you ever get over the person who broke your heart? And they never had, really. But it's funny, I think of that now, I can't believe I meant Ray. I feel like I must have meant you. I think I ought to go to bed.

EDDIE: Oh.

CAROL: I'm sorry. I think perhaps I need to go to sleep.

CAROL gets up.

I'm sorry Eddie. I'll see you in the morning.

CAROL exits. EDDIE watches after her, sitting up.

5

CAROL stands alone.

CAROL: Dear Leanne. I thought I'd send you an email as I know it's late and you'll either be out or have gone to bed, and either way you won't want a call from me. But I'm thinking of you, so I thought I'd get in touch. I wanted to say don't worry about Christmas – I completely understand. It'll be really exciting for you to spend it in another country, I've never done that, I envy you. You're very lucky to have the opportunity, I think. It'll be good for me to have a change of routine as well. Perhaps I'll go to church or something, when I was young we used to go to church on Christmas morning, and that got us out of the house. I'm sorry I reacted funny when you told me. I think I've been under some stress. Life's been very busy the last couple of weeks, I've had an old friend staying and it sends everything flying when you have a house guest, doesn't it. I didn't tell you about him because he was actually staying in your room. I hope you won't be cross. Of course, I didn't use your sheets on the bed, I used the spare set. And he's gone now, anyway, so it's nothing to worry about, and I'm getting things back to normal. Hope to hear from you soon. Love you. Mum.